Amazing Women

By Caryn Jenner

Senior Editor Caryn Jenner
Project Editor Arpita Nath
Project Art Editor Yamini Panwar
Art Editors Emma Hobson, Roohi Rais
Jacket Editor Francesca Young
Jacket Designer Amy Keast
DTP Designers Vijay Kandwal, Dheeraj Singh
Picture Researcher Sakshi Saluja
Senior Producer, Pre-Production Nikoleta Parasaki
Senior Producer Srijana Gurung
Dy. Managing Editor Vineetha Mokkil
Managing Editor Laura Gilbert
Managing Art Editors Neha Ahuja Chowdhry, Diane Peyton Jones
Art Director Martin Wilson
Publisher Sarah Larter

Reading Consultant
Jacqueline Harris

First published in Great Britain in 2017
by Dorling Kindersley Limited
80 Strand, London, WC2R 0RL

Copyright © 2017 Dorling Kindersley Limited
A Penguin Random House Company
16 17 18 19 10 9 8 7 6 5 4 3 2 1
001—298639—February/17

A CIP catalogue record for this book is available from the British Library

ISBN: 978-0-2412-8269-4

Printed and bound in China.

The publisher would also like to thank the following for their kind permission
to reproduce their photographs:
(Key: a=above, b=below/bottom, c=centre, l=left, r=right, t=top)

1 University of Washington. 3 Dorling Kindersley: Gary Ombler / Paul Stone / BAE Systems (tr). **5 Alamy Stock Photo:** EPA / Facundo Arrizabalaga. **7 Getty Images:** Tim Graham (b). **8–9 Alamy Stock Photo:** Granger Historical Picture Archive (b). **10 Getty Images:** Museum of London / Heritage Images (b). **12–13 Alamy Stock Photo:** Mike Goldwater (b). **14 Alamy Stock Photo:** Everett Collection Inc (cl). **15 Alamy Stock Photo:** Granger Historical Picture Archive (tl). **Getty Images:** PhotoQuest (clb). **17 Getty Images:** Steve Sands / WireImage. **18 Getty Images:** Jewel Samad / AFP. **20 Rex by Shutterstock:** APA-PictureDesk GmbH (t). **21 Getty Images:** Krister Soerboe / AFP (b). **23 Getty Images:** Kate Green / Anadolu Agency (t). **24–25 Rex by Shutterstock:** Universal History Archive / Universal Images Group (bc). **26 123RF.com:** Masnah Awaebueraheng (crb/Flag); Pylyp Sereda (clb/Flag). **Alamy Stock Photo:** dpa picture alliance (crb); Heritage Image Partnership Ltd (cra). **Rex by Shutterstock:** Kamal Moghrabi (clb); Sipa Press (cla). **27 123RF.com:** adamgolabek (cla/Flag); Iakov Filimonov (clb/Flag); paolo77 (crb/Flag). **Alamy Stock Photo:** Europa Newswire (clb); World History Archive (crb). **Getty Images:** A. Jones / Express (cra). **Photoshot:** (cla). **29 Getty Images:** Bettmann (b). **31 Alamy Stock Photo:** PF-(aircraft) (b). **32 Dorling Kindersley:** Gary Ombler / Paul Stone / BAE Systems (t). **33 Getty Images:** Ria Novosti / AFP (b). **35 NASA. 37 iStockphoto.com:** s-eyerkaufer (crb). **38–39 Alamy Stock Photo:** epa european pressphoto agency b.v.. **40–41 Alamy Stock Photo:** Pictorial Press Ltd (b). **42 Getty Images:** Print Collector (tl). **43 American Red Cross:** (b). **44 Alamy Stock Photo:** Photo Researchers, Inc. **46–47 123RF.com:** lifdiz. **48 University of Washington:** (b). **50 Alamy Stock Photo:** Bruce Coleman Inc. / Photoshot (cla); dpa picture alliance (crb). **Getty Images:** Nick Otto For The Washington Post (clb). **51 Alamy Stock Photo:** Photo Researchers, Inc (cla). **Getty Images:** Bertrand Rindoff Petroff (crb). **Library of Congress, Washington, D.C.:** (tr). **Rex by Shutterstock:** Richard Saker (crb). **52–53 123RF.com:** Martin Molcan (b). **53 Rex by Shutterstock:** Kristina Bumphrey / StarPix (br). **54–55 Alamy Stock Photo:** Patti McConville. **57 Getty Images:** Timothy A. Clary / AFP. **58 Rex by Shutterstock:** Universal History Archive / UIG (t). **59 123RF.com:** Evgeny Atamanenko (br). **61 Rex by Shutterstock:** maginechina (crb). **62 Rex by Shutterstock:** Universal History Archive / Universal Images Group (b). **63 Alamy Stock Photo:** Granger Historical Picture Archive (tl). **Getty Images:** Bettmann (b). **PENGUIN and the Penguin logo are trademarks of Penguin Books Ltd:** Anne Frank: The diary of a young girl by Anne Frank Cover reproduced with permission from Penguin Books Ltd. (tr). **64 Alamy Stock Photo:** dpa picture alliance archive (cla). **Getty Images:** Bettmann (cra); Hiroyuki Ito (br). **65 123RF.com:** Piotr Pawinski / ppart (clb/Frame). **Alamy Stock Photo:** Pictorial Press Ltd (crb). **Getty Images:** David Livingston (tr, clb). **Rex by Shutterstock:** Courtesy Everett Collection (cla). **66 Alamy Stock Photo:** dpa picture alliance (cla). **68 Rex by Shutterstock:** Geoff Pugh (t). **69 Alamy Stock Photo:** Reuters (b). **70–71 Getty Images:** Mandel Ngan. **72 Alamy Stock Photo:** Old Paper Studios (t). **73 Rex by Shutterstock:** (crb). **74–75 Alamy Stock Photo:** ZUMA Press, Inc.. **76 Getty Images:** Bloomberg (cra); Time Life Pictures (cla). **Rex by Shutterstock:** (clb); maginechina (crb). **77 Getty Images:** Chip Somodevilla (tl); Mint (clb). **Rex by Shutterstock:** David Fisher (tr); Ken McKay / ITV (crb). **79 Getty Images:** Kyodo News (b). **80–81 Rex by Shutterstock:** Ulander (b). **82 Rex by Shutterstock:** Melissa J. Perenson / CSM (tr). **83 Getty Images:** Phil Cole (b). **85 Getty Images:** MCT. **86–87 Getty Images:** Allsport Australi.. **88 Alamy Stock Photo:** Cal Sport Media (ca). Getty Images: Al Bello (b/l). **89 Alamy Stock Photo:** Alexander Mitrofanov (tl). **Getty Images:** Bryn Lennon (cb). **91 Alamy Stock Photo:** Patti McConville (b)

Jacket images: *Front:* **Alamy Stock Photo:** Digital Image Library clb, John Frost Newspapers; **Bridgeman Images:** PVDE cb; **Rex by Shutterstock:** Action Press crb; **Science Photo Library:** Sputnik cb/ (Valentina Tereshkova); *Back:* **akg-images:** Mondadori Portfolio / Walter Mori Angelo Cozzi, Mario De Biasi, Sergio Del Grande tl

Front Endpapers: **Getty Images:** Bryn Lennon; *Back Endpapers:* **Getty Images:** Bryn Lennon

All other images © Dorling Kindersley
For further information see: www.dkimages.com

A WORLD OF IDEAS:
SEE ALL THERE IS TO KNOW

www.dk.com

Contents

Names of women featured appear in **_bold italics_**. Glossary words appear in **bold**.

Chapter 1
Women Who Changed the World

Teenager Malala Yousafzai said, "There's a moment when you have to decide whether to be silent or to stand up." All of the women in this chapter stood up for what they believed in. They proved that one person can make a difference, big or small. Sometimes, making a difference can even change the world.

Malala Yousafzai (1997–present) just wanted to go to school, but she lived in a region of Pakistan called the Swat Valley, where a violent group called the Taliban objected to girls having an education. Along with her father, Malala spoke out against Taliban rules and became very well known in Pakistan. A member of the Taliban shot Malala when she was 15. She survived, but was badly injured. Malala and her family now live in Birmingham, England, but she continues to **campaign** for the right of girls around the world to have an education. She started the Malala Fund to bring attention to the issue, and to open schools in places around the globe wherever they are needed.

In 2014, Malala won the Nobel Peace Prize, one of the highest honours in the world. Malala says, "One child, one teacher, one book and one pen can change the world."

Malala at the official opening of the Library of Birmingham, Great Britain.

American **Helen Keller** (1880–1968) had a childhood illness that left her deaf and blind. Then Anne Sullivan came to teach her. Anne was also blind. She gave Helen a doll and spelled the word "doll" into the palm of Helen's hand so she could feel it. Soon, Helen learned more "hand words". She learned to read **braille** and to write and even to speak. Helen became the first deaf and blind person to earn a university degree. She wrote many books and articles, and worked to improve the lives of blind people. Her **autobiography** has been translated into more than 50 languages.

Helen did not let her disabilities stop her. She said, "The true test of a character is to face hard conditions with the determination to make them better."

Mother Teresa (1910–1997) changed the world by helping the poor. Born in Macedonia, she trained to be a nun at age 18. She took the name Sister Mary Teresa and became a Christian **missionary** and a teacher in the city of Calcutta (now Kolkata) in India. One day, Mother Teresa decided that she must help "the poorest of the poor". She helped whoever needed her, caring for the sick and the hungry. She also opened a school for homeless children. More volunteers joined Mother Teresa, and in 1950, she founded the Missionaries of Charity to help needy people all over the world. Mother Teresa won the Nobel Peace Prize for her work and the Catholic Church named her a saint. Today, her charity helps people in more than 130 countries.

Mother Teresa with children at her mission in Calcutta (now Kolkata), India in 1980.

In 1955, **Rosa Parks** (1913–2005) was on a bus in Alabama in the United States when the bus driver told her to move to the back of the bus so that white passengers could sit at the front. Alabama was a segregated state, which meant that black people like Rosa did not have the same rights as white people. Rosa decided to take a stand and refused to give up her seat, even though she knew she would be arrested. Her brave act inspired more people to speak out against **segregation**, such as Martin Luther King, Jr.

The historic Selma to Montgomery March in Alabama in 1965 was a major event in the American Civil Rights Movement.

They started what is known as the Civil Rights Movement, bringing attention to the cause of black people campaigning for equal rights. In 1964, the United States Civil Rights Act outlawed "**discrimination** on the basis of race, colour, religion, sex or national origin." In other words, everyone should be treated equally.

Voting in elections is an important way for people to express their opinions and fight for their rights. Yet women around the world have had to fight for this basic right to vote.

In 1903, **Emmeline Pankhurst** (1858–1928), along with her daughters, **Christabel** and **Sylvia**, organised the Women's Social and Political Union (WSPU) in Great Britain. The WSPU members, known as suffragettes, included thousands of brave and determined women from around the country. They joined in public

Suffragettes on a cart in 1909, showcasing the newspaper *Votes for Women*, which included articles written by Emmeline Pankhurst and others.

marches and protests, went to prison, and even risked their lives, so that British women could have the right to vote. In 1918, women over the age of 30 were granted the vote, but it wasn't until 1928 that all women in Great Britain received the same voting rights as men.

Zainab Salbi (1969–present) founded Women for Women International to help women survivors of war rebuild their lives and those of their children, so that future generations might live in peace. Zainab started by helping 30 women in the war-torn region of Bosnia in the early 1990s. Today, her organisation helps more than 400,000 women and their families in war zones. Born in Iraq, Zainab has also lived in the United States, the United Arab Emirates and Turkey. She currently hosts a television talk show for Arab women, which she hopes will inspire them and spread the important message of peace and understanding among all people.

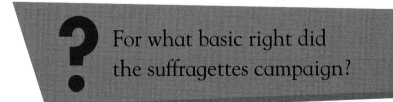

For what basic right did the suffragettes campaign?

In 1976, **Wangari Maathai** (1940–2011) joined the National Council of Women of Kenya, an organisation that aims to improve the lives of women. When women from the countryside reported that streams were drying up and that they had to walk long distances for water and firewood, Wangari realised that the problem was the loss of forests. She founded the Green Belt Movement in Kenya to encourage women

to work together to plant trees in and around their communities. The idea soon spread to other parts of Africa.

So far, the Green Belt Movement has planted more than 51 million trees, changing the lives of countless African women and helping the environment. Wangari also served in the Kenyan Parliament and won many honours, including the Nobel Peace Prize in 2004.

People planting trees in the Ethiopian countryside.

> All men and women are created equal.

American Women's Rights Convention

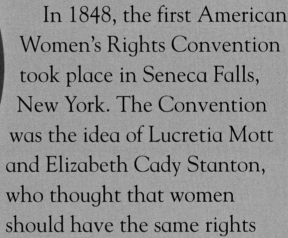

Lucretia Mott

In 1848, the first American Women's Rights Convention took place in Seneca Falls, New York. The Convention was the idea of Lucretia Mott and Elizabeth Cady Stanton, who thought that women should have the same rights as men. The 100 members of the Convention declared that "...all men and women are created equal," and that women should have the right to vote, equal education, and equal treatment under the law. It was the start of the campaign for women's rights in the United States.

Elizabeth Cady Stanton (*centre*) delivers a speech at the first American Convention on Women's Rights in Seneca Falls, New York.

Susan B. Anthony met Elizabeth Cady Stanton in 1851, and joined her as a leader in the women's rights movement.

Hooray! American women finally got the vote in 1920.

Founded in 1966, the National Organization of Women (NOW) continues to campaign for women's rights in the United States.

Chapter 2
World Leaders

These days, there are more women in positions of world power than ever before. As Hillary Clinton said, "It is past time for women to take their rightful place, side by side with men, in rooms where the fates of people, where their children's and grandchildren's fates, are decided."

In 2016, **Hillary Clinton** (1947–present) ran to be the first woman president of the United States. After studying to be a lawyer, Hillary campaigned for better education for children with disabilities. When her husband, Bill Clinton, was governor of the state of Arkansas, she worked to improve education and health care there.

In 1992, when Bill was elected president of the United States, Hillary used her role as First Lady to champion women's rights and improve health care for children across the country. She then served as a Senator for the state of New York, before running for president in 2008. When she lost to Barack Obama, Hillary became Secretary of State instead, responsible for **international relations** between the United States and other countries. Hillary says, "Always aim high, work hard and care deeply about what you believe in."

United States presidential candidate Hillary Clinton at a rally in June 2016.

Supporters of Aung San Suu Kyi made posters, such as this one, to protest her arrest.

PORT HUMAN RIGHTS

DEMOCRACY IN BUR

Aung San Suu Kyi (pronounced Ahng-Sahn-Soo-Chee) (1945–present) campaigns for honest elections and fairer laws in the country of Myanmar (formerly known as Burma) in Southeast Asia. Originally from Myanmar, Suu Kyi had settled in Great Britain with her husband and children. Then, on a visit to Myanmar in 1988, she witnessed protests against the brutal military leaders. Suu Kyi stayed to organise peaceful rallies for **democracy**, but was arrested by the government.

She spent 15 years under house arrest, which means that guards restricted her communication with the outside world and she was rarely allowed out. In 1991, she won the Nobel Peace Prize, but couldn't collect it. In 2015, thanks to Suu Kyi's determination, the National League for Democracy won Myanmar's first open election in 25 years and Suu Kyi now has a leading role in the new government.

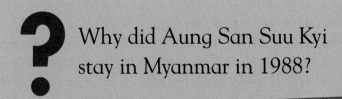

? Why did Aung San Suu Kyi stay in Myanmar in 1988?

Angela Merkel became leader of Germany in 2005.

German leader, **Angela Merkel** (1954–present), is considered one of the most powerful people in Europe. Angela grew up in what used to be known as East Germany, where she studied physics, and then worked as a scientist. Angela entered politics in 1989, when East and West Germany became one country again. She rose in German politics, and in 2005, became Germany's first woman Chancellor (leader). Germany is one of the largest and richest countries in the European Union (a group of countries in Europe whose governments work together). This means that Angela's influence reaches across the continent and around the world.

In 2006, **_Ellen Johnson Sirleaf_** (1938–present) became president of Liberia, a country in western Africa. Known for her honesty, Ellen clashed with crooked politicians while working for the Liberian Ministry of Finance in the 1980s. Ellen fled for her safety, but still worried about the situation in Liberia. What was once a relatively **prosperous** and peaceful country had become a poor, war-torn nation.

Ellen Johnson Sirleaf, president of Liberia in 2011.

In 1997, she returned and ran for president, but was forced to flee again. In 2003, Ellen returned for good and became president in 2006. She has rebuilt the country with policies such as women's rights and free primary school for children. In 2011, she was awarded the Nobel Peace Prize. Ellen faced a major challenge in 2014 when the deadly Ebola virus **epidemic** struck Liberia, but with quick action, the epidemic was halted.

For nearly 25 years, ***Sandra Day O'Connor*** (1930–present) made important decisions about American laws as one of nine justices (judges) on the United States Supreme Court. Sandra grew up on a farm in Arizona. She earned top law degrees, but no one would hire a young female lawyer in the 1950s, so she started by working for free. Sandra soon proved herself and went on to have a successful career as a lawyer and judge. In 1981, President Ronald Reagan appointed her as the first woman Supreme Court Justice. Sandra looked at legal cases on important issues such as equality and freedom. She has influenced the laws of the entire country.

In 2016, Theresa May became Great Britain's second woman Prime Minister after Margaret Thatcher.

In 2016, **Theresa May** (1956–present) became the British Prime Minister. Theresa started in politics as a local volunteer. From an early age, she had ambitions to be Prime Minister. She spent 19 years as an MP (Member of Parliament) and was Home Secretary from 2010 to 2016, responsible for policies on immigration, passports and visas, and policing in England and Wales.

As leader of Great Britain, Theresa said that her aim is to create "a country that works not for a privileged few, but for every one of us."

There have been important women leaders in history, too. **Queen Elizabeth I** (1533–1603) was Queen of England for 45 years. Although people at the time didn't expect a woman to be a strong leader, Elizabeth I proved herself to be an intelligent and able ruler.

A portrait of Elizabeth I in her coronation robes. The English ruler was extremely fond of extravagant dresses and jewellery.

During what is known as the Elizabethan Era, she defended England from invasion and increased the country's wealth and power. Elizabeth I sent explorers to the Americas, and promoted the creativity of noted writers, such as William Shakespeare.

Although **Cleopatra VII** (about 69 BCE–30 BCE) was only 17 years old when she became queen of ancient Egypt, she was a clever and highly educated ruler. Egypt was an important kingdom and other powerful nations nearby wanted to take control of it, but Cleopatra fought back. She led ancient Egypt for more than 20 years, bringing a period of peace and prosperity.

? How long did Queen Elizabeth I rule England?

Leading the Way

These are a few more of the strong and powerful women from around the world who have led their countries.

Name: Joan of Arc

Country: France

Leadership years: 1424–1431

Name: Queen Victoria

Country: Great Britain

Leadership years: 1837–1901

Name: Golda Meir

Country: Israel

Leadership years: 1969–1974

Name: Park Geun-hye

Country: South Korea

Leadership years: 2013–present

Name: Margaret Thatcher

Country: Great Britain

Leadership years: 1979–1990

Name: Portia Simpson-Miller

Country: Jamaica

Leadership years: 2006–2007;
2012–2016

Name: Benazir Bhutto

Country: Pakistan

Leadership years: 1988–1990;
1993–1996

Name: Michelle Bachelet

Country: Chile

Leadership years: 2006–2010;
2014–present

Chapter 3
Explorers

Imagine travelling to a far-off place, perhaps a place where few have ventured before. You don't know what you'll find there. You've got to be curious, brave, resourceful – and have an enormous sense of adventure!

American Indian **Sacagawea** (pronounced Sa-kuh-juh-WEE-uh) (1788–1812) had all of these qualities. In 1805, her husband, a French Canadian man, was hired as a guide on the Lewis and Clark expedition to explore the western United States. Lewis and Clark wanted Sacagawea to come too, to help them communicate with American Indians that they met along the way. She was only a teenager and had a small baby that she often carried on her back. Sacagawea soon proved that she was quick-thinking and capable. When one of the expedition boats nearly capsized, she rescued vital supplies from the rushing river. Sacagawea skillfully interpreted for the expedition team when they met American Indians from different tribes. She also taught them how to survive in the wilderness, guiding them thousands of miles across the mountains to the Pacific Ocean and back.

This painting shows Sacagawea guiding the expedition through the Rocky Mountains.

Mary Kingsley (1862–1900) lived in Victorian England. At age 30, she inherited some money and did something that was unheard of for a woman at the time. She sailed to Africa in search of adventure! In Africa, she trekked through jungles, climbed a mountain, fought off a crocodile and got caught in a tornado with a leopard. During her three trips to Africa, Mary continued to wear Victorian-style long dresses with petticoats underneath. Once, she accidentally fell into an animal trap and her petticoats saved her from the sharp stakes at the bottom! In England, Mary published books about her experiences and went on public speaking tours, telling people about Africa – the place she'd come to love.

Amelia Earhart (1897–1937) found adventure in the air. After a brief flight at an air show, Amelia decided that she had to learn to fly. She did odd jobs to pay for lessons, and bought a second-hand aeroplane. Amelia also became the first woman passenger on a flight across the Atlantic Ocean. Although this was a daring feat at the time, Amelia preferred to be the pilot instead of the passenger.

In 1932, she became the first woman to fly more than 3,200 km (2,000 miles) across the Atlantic Ocean on her own. In that same year, Amelia flew solo across North America and back, about 8,000 km (5,000 miles) in total. Five years later, she took off on her last flight. Amelia and her navigator flew about two-thirds of the way around the world – more than 35,400 km (22,000 miles)– before losing radio contact and disappearing over the Pacific Ocean. They were never found.

Amelia with a Lockheed
L-10E Electra aircraft.

Aeroplane similar to the *Gipsy Moth* flown by Amy Johnson.

Amy Johnson (1903–1941) was a record-breaking pilot from England. In 1930, she decided to fly solo from England to Australia. This was an epic journey of more than 17,700 km (11,000 miles), including stops for refuelling. Flying without a radio or navigational aids, Amy suffered through extreme heat, heavy rain and desert sandstorms, as well as exhaustion and sickness. However, 19 days later, she landed in Australia. Amy flew more record-breaking flights to different parts of the world, including the first non-stop flight across the Atlantic Ocean.

Valentina Tereshkova (1937–present) was the first woman to fly in space. She worked at a textiles factory in Russia and enjoyed parachute jumping as a hobby. **Cosmonaut** Yuri Gagarin's first ever space flight in 1961 inspired Valentina to apply for cosmonaut training. Valentina was chosen because of her experience in parachute jumping – by that time she had made 126 jumps! At the time, many people questioned whether a woman could survive in space. The training was difficult, but Valentina worked hard. In 1963, she was aboard the *Vostok* 6 spacecraft when it launched.

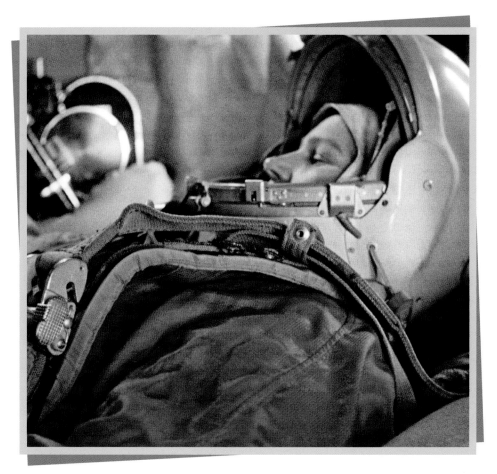

Valentina trains for a space mission, 1964.

During her three-day mission, *Vostok* 6 orbited the Earth 48 times, a distance of 1,931,213 km (1,200,000 miles).

In 1978, American **Sally Ride** (1951–2012) was studying physics at university when she was selected for the astronaut training programme with the National Aeronautics and Space Administration (NASA). In 1983, she flew aboard a NASA space shuttle as the first American woman in space. She was also the youngest American astronaut ever to go to space. Sally helped to install communication satellites and carried out experiments while orbiting the Earth. A year later, **Kathryn Sullivan** (1951–present) joined Sally on the space shuttle and became the first American woman to walk in space. Sally encouraged children's interest in science, and particularly aimed to inspire girls in the subjects of science, technology, engineering and maths.

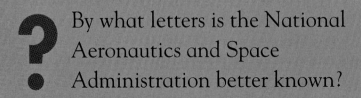

? By what letters is the National Aeronautics and Space Administration better known?

The space shuttle launches into space in 1983, with Sally Ride among the five-member crew.

Climbing Mount Everest, the world's highest mountain, is a challenging feat – especially when you're only 13 years old! **Malavath Poorna** (2000–present) from India, did just that in 2014. The activity programme that organised the Everest expedition aims to inspire young people, like Malavath, from poor backgrounds. She was chosen for the 52-day climb because of her determination and **stamina**, although she says she was afraid at first. After her 8,848-m (29,029-ft) climb, Malavath said, "Now, I feel I can do anything I set my heart to do. So can so many young girls out there. If they work towards their dream, they can make it happen."

Mount Everest

At age nine, **_Helen Thayer_** (1937–present) from New Zealand, climbed a mountain with her parents. It was 2,518 m (8,260 ft) high. Her father told her, "You don't have to climb the mountain in one long step, just one small step at a time will do it."

Since then, Helen has had all sorts of adventures, but she still remembers his advice. At age 50, she trekked 595 km (370 miles) across the Arctic Circle with her dog, Charlie. She has lived next to a pack of wolves in the Canadian wilderness, sailed down a remote stretch of the Amazon River, and trekked across the Gobi Desert in Mongolia. Now past 70, she is still planning adventures, and sharing her experiences with children.

Members of a wolf pack.

Sailing the World

At age 16, Laura Dekker was the youngest person to sail around the world on her own. Laura was born in New Zealand to Dutch parents who were living on a yacht. During her own 43,452-km (27,000-mile) voyage, completed in 2012, Laura had to deal with massive waves and near collisions with cargo ships. However, she says, "At sea, I feel comfortable and I come to rest."

Chapter 4
Science and Medicine

Women have always been at the forefront of scientific discovery – from the study of nature and the way the world works, to cutting-edge technology, to the prevention and treatment of disease and more.

Florence Nightingale (1820–1910) was determined to become a nurse, even though nursing was not considered a respectable

Florence Nightingale carries a lantern to check on injured soldiers during the Crimean War.

profession in Victorian Britain. Florence trained in Germany, and then worked in a London hospital, where she improved the dirty, **unhygienic** conditions.

She then led a team of nurses to care for injured soldiers in the Crimean War (1854–1856). The army hospital was filthy and overcrowded. Soldiers were dying, not only from war wounds, but also from infections and diseases. Florence cleaned up the hospital and gave the patients healthy food. In the evenings, she carried a lantern as she checked on the patients. She became known as "The Lady with the Lamp." After the war, Florence returned to Britain and trained nurses for the future.

Mary Seacole

Mary Seacole (1805–1881) also became a nurse during the Crimean War. She lived on the Caribbean island of Jamaica, where British soldiers often lodged with her and her mother while they recovered. Mary learned about using plants to treat illnesses and injuries, and about medicines used by the British Army. Her knowledge helped her to nurse victims of cholera and yellow fever. Mary volunteered to help British soldiers during the Crimean War, but was refused because she was black. She used her savings to travel to Crimea, where she nursed soldiers near the battlefront. Mary gave them warm, clean clothes and healthy food, often risking her life on the battlefield to help them. She looked after the soldiers so well that they called her "Mother Seacole."

American **Clara Barton** (1821–1912) was a nurse during the American Civil War (1861–1865) between the Northern and Southern states. At first, Clara looked after wounded soldiers at a hospital in the capital, Washington, D.C., but then she decided she would be more useful near the battlefront. Clara gathered supplies in a wagon led by a mule and travelled from battlefield to battlefield, bringing supplies wherever they were needed, and nursing the soldiers. The grateful soldiers called her the "Angel of the Battlefield."

After the war, Clara set up an organisation to search for missing soldiers. She also travelled to Europe, where she learned about an international charity called the Red Cross. In 1881, she founded the American Red Cross, which has provided care to millions of people across the United States ever since.

The symbol of the American Red Cross.

Marie performs an experiment
into radioactivity.

Born in Poland, **Marie Curie** (1867–1934) is best known for her research into fighting cancer. Marie moved to France to study mathematics and physics. She investigated the invisible **radioactive** rays given off by a chemical element called uranium. Along with her husband, Pierre Curie, Marie discovered two new chemical elements, polonium and radium, and won the Nobel Prize for Physics in 1903. Marie continued her research into radioactivity and in 1911, won the Nobel Prize for Chemistry. She is the only person ever to win the Nobel Prize for both physics and chemistry. Thanks to Marie Curie's pioneering work, doctors can now use radioactivity to treat cancer.

? For which two branches of science did Marie Curie win the Nobel Prize?

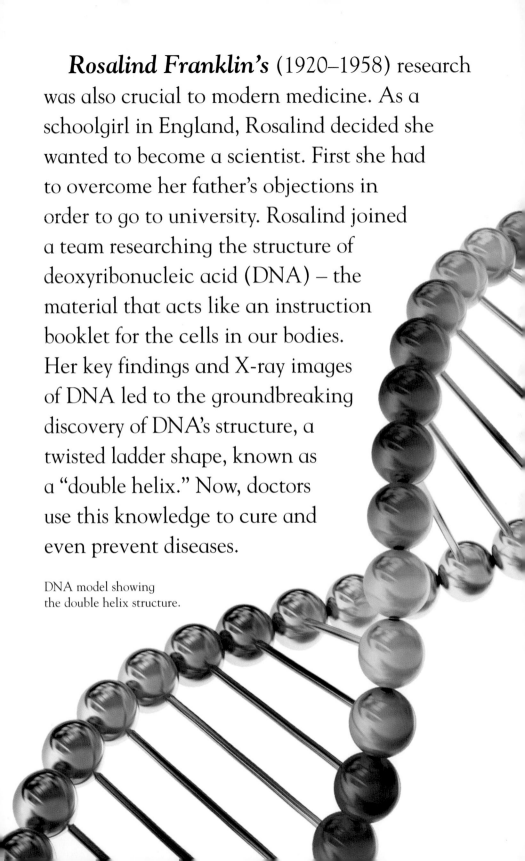

Rosalind Franklin's (1920–1958) research was also crucial to modern medicine. As a schoolgirl in England, Rosalind decided she wanted to become a scientist. First she had to overcome her father's objections in order to go to university. Rosalind joined a team researching the structure of deoxyribonucleic acid (DNA) – the material that acts like an instruction booklet for the cells in our bodies. Her key findings and X-ray images of DNA led to the groundbreaking discovery of DNA's structure, a twisted ladder shape, known as a "double helix." Now, doctors use this knowledge to cure and even prevent diseases.

DNA model showing
the double helix structure.

Ada Lovelace (1815–1852) is known as the "first computer programmer". The daughter of famous English poet, Lord Byron, Ada enjoyed studying mathematics and learning about new inventions of the Industrial Revolution, such as steam engines. She even drew up plans for a flying machine. At age 17, Ada met mathematician Charles Babbage, who had written plans for a complicated device called an "**Analytical Engine**". Ada expanded on his ideas, adding her own step-by-step description of operations, similar to what we now call "coding". She also realised that the device could have many uses beyond mathematics. Although the Analytical Engine was never built, Ada was ahead of her time, imagining a future full of computers!

Robotics expert **Yoky Matsuoka** (1972–present) is one of many scientists today who is taking Ada Lovelace's early work in computer technology to new levels. Originally from Japan, Yoky moved to the United States as a teenager. A keen tennis player, she initially wanted to invent a robot that could play tennis! This interest led Yoky to develop a robotic arm, and to use robotics to help people regain movement in disabled limbs.

Yoky tests the robotic arm that she invented.

She has been a professor of robotics, and helped to establish Google's research laboratory to find new ways of using computer technology. Yoky now develops cutting-edge health-related advances for Apple Inc., the technology company.

Chinese astronomer **Wang Zhenyi** (pronounced Wang jen-YEE) (1768–1797) studied the relationships between the Earth, the Sun and the Moon. She wrote a scientific paper explaining why people don't fall off the Earth even though it's round. This was an early description of the force of gravity. She also explained that a lunar eclipse occurs when the Earth blocks the sunlight from reaching the Moon. She made a model eclipse using a lamp, a table and a mirror to represent the Sun, the Earth and the Moon. This theory also proved to be correct.

Even in the 18th century, Zhenyi promoted equality in science. She declared that men and women "are all people, who have the same reason for studying". There is a crater on the planet Venus named in her honour.

Super Scientists

Here are a few more women who are super scientists, investigating the world around us and improving our lives.

Jane Goodall (1934–present)
British primatologist, studies chimpanzees in the wild.

Jennifer Doudna (1964–present) and **Emmanuelle Charpentier** (1968–present)

American and French microbiologists, pioneered a technique for changing DNA (called "gene editing"), leading to new medical breakthroughs.

Lise Meitner (1878–1968)

Austrian physicist, discovered a key chemical process called nuclear fission.

Grace Hopper (1906–1992)

American computer scientist, developed early computer languages.

Hualan Chen (1969–present)

Chinese virologist, researches flu viruses, leading to new vaccines.

Maggie Aderin-Pocock (1968–present)

British space scientist, designs space telescopes and satellites.

Chapter 5
Writers, Artists and Performers

Throughout history, women have expressed themselves through creative endeavours. The drive to write, paint, play music, dance, or do any other creative activity, can be powerful. As the author, J.K. (Joanne) Rowling, says, "I'll be writing until I can't write anymore. It's a **compulsion** with me. I love writing."

British sensation **J.K. Rowling** (1965–present) wrote the best-selling Harry Potter books. The idea of the young wizard came to her during a train ride in 1990, and she spent the next several years planning Harry's adventures. Jo, as she's known, often went to a local café in Edinburgh, Scotland, to write. Once she finished writing the first story, Jo needed a publisher to make it into a book for the public to read. Believe it or not, 12 publishers turned down Harry Potter. Jo did not give up, and in 1997, *Harry Potter and the Philosopher's Stone* was published in Great Britain. In 1998, it was published in the US, where the title was *Harry Potter and the Sorcerer's Stone*. The seven Harry Potter books have now sold more than 450 million copies in 78 languages around the world. Jo currently writes detective books for adults using a **pen name**.

J.K. Rowling's hero, Harry Potter, travels to Hogwarts School of Witchcraft and Wizardry on a steam train similar to this one. J.K. Rowling (*inset*) author of the Harry Potter series.

The **Brontë** sisters – **Charlotte** (1816–1855), **Emily** (1818–1848), and **Anne** (1820–1849) – wrote exciting novels featuring strong female characters. Their books have become famous classics. Charlotte is best known for *Jane Eyre*, Emily for *Wuthering Heights* and Anne for *The Tenant of Wildfell Hall*. The sisters grew up in a remote part of the Yorkshire moors in England. Even as children, they enjoyed writing stories and poetry. The sisters weren't sure if female writers would be taken seriously, so they initially published their writing using pen names – Currer Bell for Charlotte, Ellis Bell for

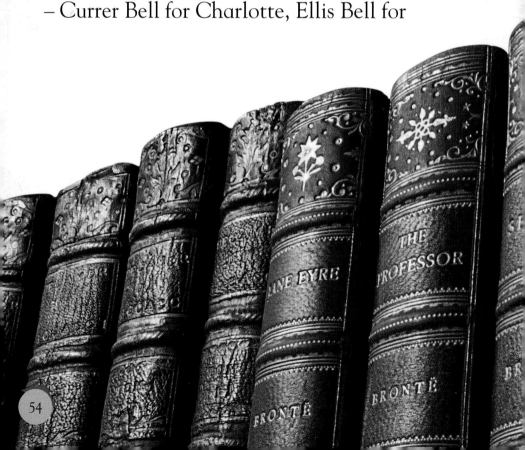

Emily and Acton Bell for Anne. By the time the sisters revealed their true identities, their books were already hugely successful – and they have stood the test of time.

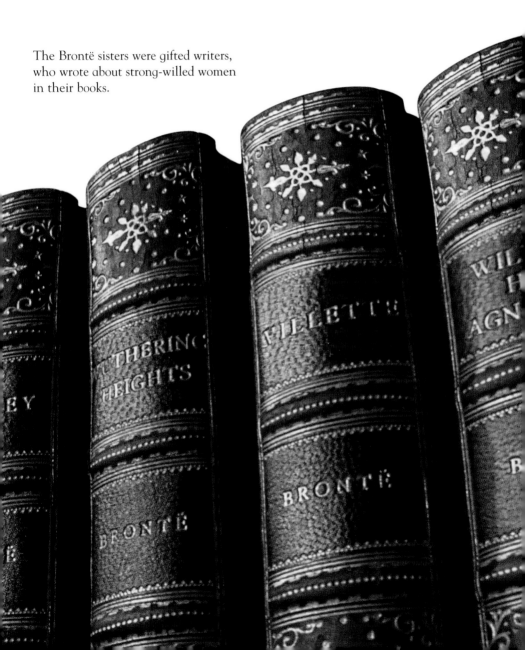

The Brontë sisters were gifted writers, who wrote about strong-willed women in their books.

Like her most famous character, Anne of Green Gables, **L.M. Montgomery** (1874–1942), grew up on Prince Edward Island in Canada. Named Lucy Maud, she kept a journal and wrote poetry from an early age. Lucy Maud became a teacher, but continued to write poems and stories, some of which were published in magazines. Publishers initially turned down her first novel, *Anne of Green Gables*, but it was finally published in 1908 and became a bestseller.

Lucy Maud wrote more novels about the lively, strong-minded character of Anne. She also wrote many other books, short stories, poems and articles. Most of her writing describes life on her beloved Prince Edward Island.

A woman of many talents, **Maya Angelou** (1928–2014) is best known as a writer. She wrote several volumes of her autobiography, as well as poetry, essays and children's books. She also performed as a singer and actress, and wrote and directed plays and movies. Maya and her brother were raised by their grandmother in the southern United States at a time when black people did not have the same rights as white people. Maya campaigned for civil rights so that everyone would be treated equally. Maya wrote, "Beneath the skin, beyond the differing features, and into the true heart of being, fundamentally, we are more alike, my friend, than we are unalike."

Maya giving a speech in 2004.

Summertime, painted by Mary Cassatt in 1894.

Mary Cassatt (1844–1926) wanted to be respected as a serious artist at a time when art was considered a "hobby" for women, not a career. Born to a wealthy American family, Mary spent most of her adult life in Paris, France. A French painter named Edgar Degas invited her to exhibit with the Impressionists. These were artists who used broad strokes of colour to capture the overall impression of a scene, rather than the more traditional, realistic style of painting. Mary became known for her Impressionist paintings of women, especially mothers with children. She experimented with different techniques, such as pastels and print-making. Mary's work is now worth millions of pounds, and can be seen in galleries around the world.

As a child in Russia, **Anna Pavlova** (1881–1931) was enchanted by the ballet *The Sleeping Beauty*. At the age of ten, she was accepted to the Imperial Ballet School. She then worked her way up to become prima ballerina (main dancer). Her most famous role was in the ballet *The Dying Swan*. However, what Anna enjoyed most was travelling to perform for people around the globe, introducing them to the beauty of ballet. She formed her own dance company to tour the world.

Anna Pavlova helped to develop pointe shoes, which enable ballerinas to dance on their toes.

Anna combined elements of traditional dances of countries she visited into her ballets. Her dance company performed in both big cities and small towns, inspiring new generations to enjoy the magic of ballet.

Born in Scotland, musician ***Evelyn Glennie*** (1965–present) plays percussion instruments, such as different kinds of drums, xylophones, cymbals, and chimes, as well as unusual objects such as pots and pans, stones, and even parts of cars. Percussion means that she hits the instruments, either with her hands, or with drumsticks, or with another object, to make music. In fact, Evelyn has been almost completely deaf since the age of 12. She says, "Losing my hearing meant learning how to listen differently." Instead of listening to the music with her ears, Evelyn feels the vibrations of the sounds with her body. She feels the vibrations best when she performs barefoot. Evelyn says her aim is to "teach the world to listen".

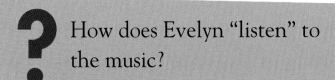

? How does Evelyn "listen" to the music?

Evelyn in 2001 with part of her collection of more than 2,000 percussion instruments.

Anne Frank

During World War II, teenager **Anne Frank** (1929–1945) kept a diary while in hiding from the Nazis, who were **persecuting** Jewish people like the Frank family. Anne, her sister and her parents were in grave danger. They hid for two years until the Nazis discovered them and sent them to a concentration camp to be tortured. Only Anne's father survived. *The Diary of a Young Girl* is about the hardships and dangers they faced, but also about Anne's hopes for **tolerance** and peace in the future. Remarkably, Anne remained optimistic despite the risk of being captured.

Anne Frank at her home in Amsterdam, the Netherlands, before the family went into hiding in 1942.

The Frank family and four other people hid in the Secret Annex, part of a building in Amsterdam. They couldn't go outside for fear of being discovered.

Anne Frank

After World War II, Anne's father, Otto Frank, shows how a bookcase covered the entrance to the Secret Annex.

Creative Women

Here is a small selection of creative women who have contributed to the arts – from literature and painting, to music and movies!

Adele Adkins (1988–present) British singer-songwriter, known for modern hits such as "Rolling in the Deep", "Skyfall" and "Hello".

Frida Kahlo (1907–1954) Mexican painter best known for her self-portraits.

Yuja Wang (1987–present) Chinese musician who travels around the world giving piano concerts.

Audrey Hepburn (1929–1993) Belgian actress famous for classic movies such as *Breakfast at Tiffany's* and *My Fair Lady*. She was also a Goodwill Ambassador for UNICEF.

Judy Blume (1938–present) American writer known for her books for children and teenagers such as *Superfudge* and *Are You There God? It's Me, Margaret.*

Margaret Atwood (1939–present) Canadian writer whose many novels include *Cat's Eye*, *The Handmaid's Tale* and the *MaddAddam* trilogy.

Ella Fitzgerald (1917–1996) American jazz singer known as "The First Lady of Song", famous for hits such as "A-Tisket, A-Tasket" and "Love is Here to Stay."

Chapter 6
Business Leaders

The products and services that we use every day exist thanks to many kinds of businesses. Although there are more women in business now than ever before, most of the top jobs are still taken by men. As Sheryl Sandberg says, "Real change will come when powerful women are less of an exception."

Sheryl with the German edition of her book in 2013.

As Chief Operating Officer (COO) at Facebook, the popular social networking site, **Sheryl Sandberg** (1969–present) has one of the top Internet jobs in the world. At Facebook, she is in charge of the day-to-day business of the company. Her past experience includes working for the World Bank, the United States Department of Treasury, and the Internet search engine, Google.

Sheryl encourages women to be ambitious and to pursue leadership positions in business. In 2013, she wrote *Lean In: Women, Work, and the Will to Lead*, and started Lean In Circles around the world, where groups of women meet to support and encourage each other. Sheryl says, "Feeling confident – or pretending that you feel confident – is necessary to reach for opportunities."

As a child in Britain, **Martha Lane Fox** (1973–present) had an ambition to run a hotel. Instead, she became an Internet **entrepreneur** at the age of 25, founding lastminute.com – Europe's top travel and leisure website. Martha then became the British government's UK Digital Champion responsible for expanding online access and training.

Martha visits a museum exhibition about the Internet in 2014.

In 2013, she was appointed to the House of Lords at the British Parliament, specialising in issues related to digital technology, such as online safety. She currently runs doteveryone.org.uk – a digital organisation that aims to share information and skills so that the Internet benefits as many people as possible. Martha is on the board of directors of several companies, including Twitter, Marks & Spencer and the television network, Channel 4.

Arianna Huffington (1950–present)
launched *The Huffington Post* website in 2005.
Since then, it has become one of the world's
most widely read news and blogging websites.
It has also won the prestigious Pulitzer Prize for
journalism in the USA. In 2011, Arianna sold
The Huffington Post to Internet giant AOL,
earning about $21 million. She continued to run
The Huffington Post until 2016, when she founded
Thrive Global, a new website focusing on health
and lifestyle issues.

Born in Greece, Arianna also spent time in
England before moving to the United States.
She has written 15 books on a variety of subjects.

Arianna aims to "inform, inspire, entertain and empower" people
through *The Huffington Post*.

Oprah Winfrey (1954–present) is one of the world's most influential women. As well as being queen of the TV talk show, Oprah owns her own television network, film and TV production company, magazines and more. Despite a difficult childhood, moving between her mother, father, and grandmother, Oprah did well at school. Her special talent

was speaking. After winning a competition, she was offered a job at a radio station. Oprah went on to become a news reporter, and then a talk show host. *The Oprah Winfrey Show* aired on TV for 25 years, and was one of the top-rated talk shows in the United States. Oprah contributes some of her estimated $3.2 billion fortune towards good causes. She says, "It doesn't matter who you are, where you come from. The ability to triumph begins with you – always."

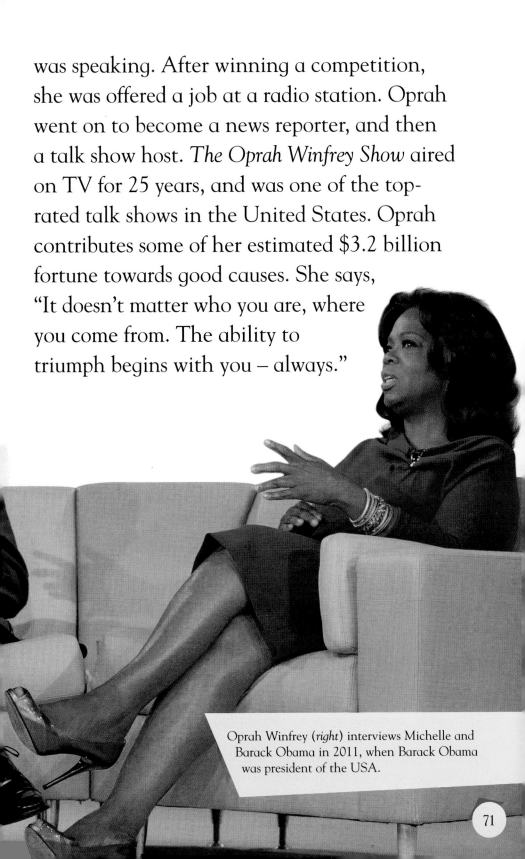

Oprah Winfrey (*right*) interviews Michelle and Barack Obama in 2011, when Barack Obama was president of the USA.

A 1940s advertisement for one of Madam C.J. Walker's hair products.

Born Sarah Breedlove to parents who were former slaves, **Madam C.J. Walker** (1867–1919) became the first female African-American millionaire. In those days, hair loss and scalp complaints were common. Sarah experimented with home remedies, and developed her own hair treatment, especially for black women. Using her then-husband's name, she called it "Madam Walker's Wonderful Hair Grower". She created a range of hair products with distinctive packaging, sold them door-to-door, and gave sales demonstrations throughout the southern United States. A sharp businesswoman,

Sarah trained other women to sell her products, and expanded her business to the Caribbean islands. With much of the money she earned, Sarah gave back to the African-American community who had contributed to her success.

In 1976, **Anita Roddick** (1942–2007) opened The Body Shop's first store in Brighton, England. Her ambition was simply to earn a living – but in a way that promoted **fair trade**, protected the environment, and opposed animal testing.

The Body Shop was one of the first companies to raise awareness of **ethical** issues. Anita travelled around the world, learning about natural ingredients to put in her bath and beauty products. Today, there are more than

Anita showcases some of The Body Shop's products in 1978.

3,000 shops in 63 countries around the world. In 2006, Anita sold The Body Shop to the L'Oreal Group, with the agreement that they would continue to uphold Anita's ethical principles.

A model wears an evening dress from Chanel's 1963 collection.

The House of Chanel is a world-famous fashion label. Created in 1913 by the French designer **Coco Chanel** (1883–1971), the label includes clothes, accessories and perfumes. Coco started by making and selling hats in Paris. She then added a line of women's clothing, by creating garments using a soft jersey fabric that was much more comfortable than the rigid corsets of the past. Coco's flair for designing wearable, fashionable clothes helped her to move with the times, and her label flourished. Today, the **legacy** of Coco Chanel continues, with new generations influenced by the classic Chanel style.

? How did Coco Chanel start her business?

Business Brains

These are some of the many women who have made an impact on the world of business.

Helena Rubinstein
1872–1965

Founder of international cosmetics company that bears her name.

Phuti Mahanyele
1971–present

Financial whizz who runs her own investment company in South Africa.

Ursula Burns
1958–present

Head of Xerox, one of the world's top business services companies.

Cher Wang
1958–present

Co-founder and head of HTC, maker of smartphones and other mobile devices.

Janet Yellen
1946–present

Influential head of the Federal Reserve, the central bank of the USA.

Joy Mangano
1956–present

Inventor whose Miracle Mop and other household gadgets made her a millionaire.

Chanda Kochhar
1961–present

Head of India's biggest bank and president of the International Monetary Conference.

Karren Brady
1969–present

Runs a leading British football club and advises on business issues in the House of Lords.

Chapter 7
Sports Sensations

These days women can participate in any sport they choose, though this was not always the case. Women have only been allowed to compete in the Olympic Games since 1900. Being an amazing sportsperson takes a lot of practice and dedication.

With her powerful playing style, tennis star **Serena Williams** (1981–present) has been at the top of the sport for nearly 20 years. She's famous for her fierce determination and her pure enjoyment of a good match. The youngest of five sisters, Serena was four when she began playing tennis in the United States. Serena and her sister, **Venus** (1980–present), started playing professionally as teenagers, often in matches against each other. They have also won many tournaments as doubles partners. To date, Serena has won more than 70 singles titles and 23 doubles titles. She and her sister Venus have also won four Olympic gold medals in women's doubles.

Off the court, Serena has her own fashion brand. She is also a UNICEF Goodwill Ambassador, and uses her Serena Williams Fund to build schools in Kenya, support equality in education and help people affected by violence.

Venus and Serena in action at the women's doubles finals of the 2016 Wimbledon tournament.

Janica Kostelic (1982–present) first tried skiing when she was three years old. By age nine, she was skiing in races. Janica's parents drove her and her brother, who was also a skier, from their home in Croatia to races all over Europe. Rather than stay in hotels, the family often slept in a tent or in the car to save money. At age 16, Janica entered the 1998 Winter Olympics, finishing in 8th place. A few years later, disaster hit when Janica crashed during training and injured her right knee. She recovered, but then injured

Janica in action at the World Alpine Ski Championships in 2003.

her left knee. Janica refused to give up. By the 2002 Winter Olympics, she was skiing in top form, winning three gold medals and one silver. Janica won more medals at the 2006 Olympics. Her nickname is the "Croatian Sensation"!

In the 1960s, American **Wilma Rudolph** (1940–1994) was known as "the world's fastest woman". However, as a child, she had a serious illness called polio, and had to wear a metal brace on her leg. With the help of physical therapy, Wilma was running and playing with her 21 brothers and sisters by the time she was 12. She especially loved to play basketball. Her coach called her "Skeeter" because she was little, fast and always getting in the way like a mosquito. Wilma also trained with the track team. She was a particularly speedy sprinter, winning a bronze medal at the 1956 Olympics, and three gold medals at the 1960 Olympics. She established the Wilma Rudolph Foundation to help other athletes, especially African-American women like herself. Wilma said, "The most important aspect is to be yourself and have confidence in yourself."

American gymnast **_Simone Biles_** (1997–present) was the star of the 2016 Olympic Games, winning four gold medals and one bronze medal. Even before her Olympic success, she already had 14 World Championship

Simone performs at the P&G Championships in 2016.

medals, including gold for all-round gymnast three years in a row.

Simone and her sister were young children when their parents adopted them. When Simone was six, her daycare group visited a gymnastics training center, where coaches spotted her talent. Simone's years of training have helped her learn to overcome competition nerves. Now 19, she performs on the vault, balance beam, uneven bars, and her favourite, the floor routine. Simone might be small, but her flips, twists, and handsprings are so high, they seem to defy gravity!

Tanni Grey-Thompson (1969–present) is a wheelchair racer. Born in Wales, Tanni always loved sport, despite having a condition called spina bifida, which means that she can't walk. Inspired by watching the London Marathon on TV, Tanni started wheelchair racing at the age of 13. Her grandfather told her to "aim high, even if you hit a cabbage". He meant that she should keep aiming for her goals and not give up.

Tanni at the 2004 Paralympic Games, where she won the gold medal.

Tanni broke 30 world records, won six London marathons and a total of 11 gold medals in the Paralympics – the Olympic Games for disabled athletes. She has also received many honours, such as becoming a member of the House of Lords at the British Parliament, where she specialises in issues relating both to sport and disabilities. She continues to aim high in life.

As a child, **Angela James** (1964–present) was the top scorer in the boys' ice hockey league in Toronto, Canada. The next year, however, girls were banned from playing in the boys' league. Angela knew that she was at least as good as the boys – and better than most of them. She started playing for a girls' ice hockey league, and just got better and better. She was a tough, determined player with a talent for scoring goals. Angela led the Canadian women's team to many spectacular wins, including four gold medals in the World Championships. In 2010, she was honored by the Hockey Hall of Fame in Toronto. Angela now runs an ice hockey school and continues to encourage women in sport.

Angela playing for the Canadian national team.

Layne Beachley (1972–present) loves to surf. She's also determined to win. Adopted as a baby, Layne grew up near the beaches of Sydney in Australia. She started surfing when she was four years old, and at age seven decided she wanted to become a champion surfer. Layne competed in her first professional surfing competition at age 16. Her training and focus paid off when she became the only surfer ever to win the World Championship six years in a row, from 1998 to 2003. Although troubled by illness, Layne won her seventh World Championship in 2006 through hard work and determination. Layne's aim now is to support other women in achieving their dreams. Her dream is to keep surfing until she's at least 80.

Layne in action during the
Roxy Fiji Surf Jam in 2001.

Women in **SPORTS**

Football

The United States women's football team plays the Korean Republic in 2013. Around the world, more than 29 million girls and women play football, from local children's leagues up to international level.

Swimming

China's Ye Shiwen was only 16 years old when she won two gold medals at the 2012 Olympics. Here, she swims the butterfly stroke in the 200 m medley at the 2013 World Championships.

Basketball

Dynamo Moscow women's basketball team from Russia plays Maccabi Ashdod from Israel in 2014. Shooting hoops is a fast, exciting game, and participation in women's basketball is on the rise.

Cycling

Winning cyclists Katie Archibald, Elinor Barker, Laura Trott, and Joanna Rowsell of Great Britain display their gold medals at the 2014 Track Cycling World Championships. The same team broke the world record at the 2016 Olympic Games.

Amazing Women Quiz

See if you can find the answers to these questions about what you have read.

1. Who said, "One child, one teacher, one book and one pen can change the world"?

2. Who was the first deaf and blind person to earn a university degree?

3. Who campaigns for honest elections and fairer laws in the country of Myanmar?

4. Angela Merkel became Chancellor (leader) of which country in 2005?

5. During her three-day space mission on board the *Vostok* 6, who orbited the Earth 48 times?

6. Which mountain did teenager Malavath Poorna climb?

7. Which two women nursed soldiers during the Crimean War?

8. Who is known as the "first computer programmer"?

9. Who developed a robotic arm?

10. Who wrote the Harry Potter books?

11. Which three sisters wrote exciting novels featuring strong female characters?

12. Which businesswoman wrote a book called *Lean In: Women, Work and the Will to Lead*?

13. Who was known as "the world's fastest woman"?

14. Who was inspired to race by watching the London Marathon on TV?

Answers on page 93.

Glossary

Analytical
Relating to the detailed study of something.

Autobiography
Book written about the author's own life.

Braille
System of raised dots for blind people to read using their sense of touch.

Campaign
Take a series of actions towards a particular goal.

Compulsion
Feeling as if you must do something.

Cosmonaut
Russian (or Soviet) astronaut.

Democracy
Government in which the people have the power to vote.

Discrimination
Treating some people unfairly.

Entrepreneur
Someone who starts their own business.

Epidemic
Outbreak of a disease that spreads quickly.

Ethical
Honest and responsible; concern for issues such as the environment and fair trade.

Fair trade
Paying all workers a decent wage.

International relations
Relationships between countries.

Legacy
Ideas or things that are passed on to the future.

Missionary
Person sent to do religious and social work.

Pen name
Made-up name used by an author.

Persecute
To treat people badly because of their race or religion or political beliefs.

Prosperous
Rich, successful.

Radioactive
Powerful and often dangerous energy given off by certain materials.

Segregation
Policy of separating people by race and treating them differently.

Stamina
Long-lasting energy.

Tolerance
Acceptance of people who are different from you.

Unhygienic
Dirty and unhealthy.

Answers to the Amazing Women Quiz:

1. Malala Yousafzai **2.** Helen Keller **3.** Aung San Suu Kyi
4. Germany **5.** Valentina Tereshkova **6.** Mount Everest
7. Florence Nightingale and Mary Seacole **8.** Ada Lovelace
9. Yoky Matsuoka **10.** J.K. Rowling **11.** Charlotte, Emily, and Anne Brontë **12.** Sheryl Sandberg **13.** Wilma Rudolph
14. Tanni Grey-Thompson

Guide for Parents

DK Readers is a four-level interactive reading adventure series for children, developing the habit of reading widely for both pleasure and information. These chapter books have an exciting main narrative interspersed with a range of reading genres to suit your child's reading ability, as required by the National Curriculum. Each book is designed to develop your child's reading skills, fluency, grammar awareness, and comprehension in order to build confidence and engagement when reading.

Ready for a *Reading Alone* book

YOUR CHILD SHOULD

- be able to read independently and silently for extended periods of time.
- read aloud flexibly and fluently, in expressive phrases with the listener in mind.
- respond to what they are reading with an enquiring mind.

A VALUABLE AND SHARED READING EXPERIENCE

Supporting children when they are reading proficiently can encourage them to value reading and to view reading as an interesting, purposeful, and enjoyable pastime. So here are a few tips on how to use this book with your child.

TIP 1 Reading aloud as a learning opportunity:

- if your child has already read some of the book, ask him/her to explain the earlier part briefly.
- encourage your child to read slightly slower than his/her normal silent reading speed so that the words are clear and the listener has time to absorb the information, too.

Reading aloud provides your child with practice in expressive reading and performing to a listener, as well as a chance to share his/her responses to the narrative and the information.

TIP 2 Praise, share and chat

- encourage your child to recall specific details after each chapter.
- provide opportunities for your child to pick out interesting words and discuss what they mean.
- discuss how the author captures the reader's interest, or how effective the non-fiction layouts are.
- ask the questions provided on some pages and in the quiz. These help to develop comprehension skills and awareness of the language used.
- ask if there's anything that your child would like to discover more about.

Further information can be researched in the index of other non-fiction books or on the Internet.

A FEW ADDITIONAL TIPS

- Continue to read to your child regularly to demonstrate fluency, phrasing and expression; to find out or check information; and for sharing enjoyment.
- Encourage your child to read a range of different genres, such as newspapers, poems, review articles and instructions.
- Provide opportunities for your child to read to a variety of eager listeners, such as a sibling or a grandparent.

Index